W9-BYZ-315

Children's Authors

Gertrude Chandler Warner

Jill C. Wheeler
ABDO Publishing Company

visit us at
www.abdopub.com

Published by ABDO Publishing Company, 4940 Viking Drive, Edina, Minnesota 55435.
Copyright © 2005 by Abdo Consulting Group, Inc. International copyrights reserved in all
countries. No part of this book may be reproduced in any form without written permission from
the publisher. The Checkerboard Library™ is a trademark and logo of ABDO Publishing
Company.

Printed in the United States.

Cover Photo: Elizabeth J. Noonan
Interior Photos: Aspinock Historical Society pp. 15, 19; Corbis p. 8; Fotosearch p. 12; Gertrude
    C. Warner materials used with permission of Elizabeth J. Noonan pp. 4, 5, 7, 11, 13, 17,
    23; Getty Images p. 9

Editors: Megan Murphy, Kristin Van Cleaf
Art Direction: Neil Klinepier

Library of Congress Cataloging-in-Publication Data

Wheeler, Jill C., 1964-
    Gertrude Chandler Warner / Jill C. Wheeler.
       p. cm. -- (Children's authors)
    Includes bibliographical references (p.) and index.
    ISBN 1-59197-609-X
       1. Warner, Gertrude Chandler, 1890---Juvenile literature. 2. Authors, American--20th
century--Biography--Juvenile literature. 3. Children's stories--Authorship--Juvenile
literature. [1. Warner, Gertrude Chandler, 1890- 2. Authors, American. 3. Women--Biography.]
I. Title. II. Series.

PS3545.A738Z93 2004
813'.52--dc22
[B]
                                                                              2003063842

Contents

Gertrude Chandler Warner

As a young girl, Gertrude Chandler Warner loved tea parties. When she was nine years old, she would stay after school and have tea in the school yard. Her mother asked her why she kept coming home late. Gertrude told her it was because she was writing a book.

Her mother asked to see the book. So, Gertrude had to write something quickly. She composed her own story about a well-known character visiting the zoo. She used watercolors to paint the pictures. She named it *Golliwogg at the Zoo.*

*Gertrude wrote her first book when she was nine. **Golliwogg at the Zoo** was a gift to her grandfather.*

Gertrude had written her first book. She gave it to her grandfather for Christmas. The following year, she wrote another book for her grandmother. These stories were only the first of many Gertrude would write in her lifetime.

Today, Gertrude Chandler Warner is best known for writing The Boxcar Children mystery series. Millions of people around the world enjoy these books, as well as Gertrude's many other stories.

Gertrude Chandler Warner

Growing Up in Putnam

Gertrude Chandler Warner was born on April 16, 1890, in Putnam, Connecticut. She had an older sister named Frances and a younger brother, John. Her house was across the tracks from the busy train **depot**. The Warner children often watched the trains go by the house.

Gertrude's father, Edgar, was a judge in Putnam. Her mother, Jane, led the town school committee. Both parents were very involved in the community.

From a young age, Gertrude had an active imagination. She loved playing with her dollhouse. She called the dolls that lived there Mr. and Mrs. Delight. She also loved reading. Her favorite book was *Alice in Wonderland* by Lewis Carroll.

Gertrude and Frances enjoyed writing poems and stories. Jane encouraged her daughters by buying them ten-cent notebooks to write in.

Gertrude was an active child, but she was sick a lot. She had many sore throats and was often sneezing. Eventually, poor health forced Gertrude to drop out of high school. Her mother and a **tutor** helped her with her studies. Even so, Gertrude never graduated.

The Warner Family (from left) Edgar, Frances, John, Gertrude, and Jane

Unlikely Teacher

Warner published her first book in 1916, when she was 26 years old. In *House of Delight*, Warner described her experiences with her beloved dollhouse. She also wrote stories and articles for local magazines.

In 1917, the United States entered **World War I**. Warner decided to join the **Red Cross.** She helped with publicity.

Red Cross workers help a young boy during a flood.

The war effort pulled many people away from their jobs and homes. By 1918, Israel Putnam School did not have enough teachers. The local school board knew Warner had been a Sunday school teacher for her church. They asked her if she would help teach first grade, and she agreed.

Warner was unsure about teaching, however. Most teachers attend college to prepare for the job. She had never even graduated from high school. Warner found this work very different from teaching Sunday school. But she discovered she liked it.

Opposite page: *During World War I, the Red Cross launched a special campaign to reach more volunteers. Warner, not pictured, was active in the Red Cross most of her life.*

More Stories

Even as a teacher, Warner still made writing a priority. She lived with her parents, and her mother often gave her ideas for stories.

Once, Jane suggested Gertrude write about nature. The stories appeared in *Little Folks* magazine. Warner also composed a collection of stories about the stars. They later appeared in a book called *Star Stories*.

Children enjoyed Warner's writing. She wrote in a way that was easy to understand. Gertrude and Frances also published many articles in magazines for adults. Some of those articles later appeared in a book. It was called *Life's Minor Collisions*.

By this time, Warner had published 11 books. She had written many articles for newspapers and magazines, too. She was used to writing what other people asked her to write. But that was about to change.

The Warner family often played music together when Gertrude (left) and Frances were growing up. Gertrude later learned to play the organ.

A Story of Her Own

Warner was often sick, even as an adult. One day, she was home with **bronchitis**. She was thinking about writing something to make herself feel better. She remembered peeking into a caboose as a child. She had seen a small stove, a coffeepot, and some cups inside.

Soon, Warner was imagining a story about children living in a train car. That was how *The Boxcar Children* began. She created a story about four orphan children. Their names were Henry, Jessie, Violet, and Benny Alden. The **manuscript** was published in 1924.

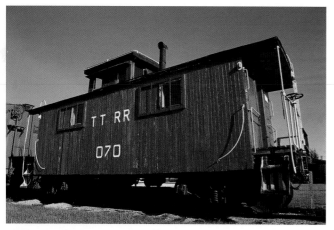

Some grown-ups did not like *The Boxcar Children* when it first came out. They did not think children should live without parents. But young readers loved the idea.

The caboose is usually the last car of a train. It is often where the train's crew lives.

Years later, Warner had a chance to ride inside a caboose. She was thrilled to see it was much as she had imagined it.

Warner's mother once told her she would never make money as a writer. By the time she was 34, however, she had written about a dozen books.

Writer and Teacher

In 1932, Warner was in a car accident. She broke her back and nearly died. She had to stay in bed and rest. Once again, being **bedridden** gave her time to write.

Soon after the accident, Warner published a series of books about children from different backgrounds. The first book was titled *The World in a Barn*. She and Frances also wrote more articles for adults.

Like most teachers, Warner had summers to herself. She spent two summers working for a publisher in Chicago, Illinois. This encouraged her to rewrite *The Boxcar Children* to make it easier to read.

Warner also attended Yale University in New Haven, Connecticut, for several summers. She took classes there to help her become a better teacher.

However, Warner was already a good teacher. She came up with special activities for her students. She even had surprises for birthdays and rainy days.

Warner taught first grade at Israel Putnam School. She would often ask her students for advice on how to make her writing better.

More Time to Write

Warner spent the next few years writing more books for children and adults. One of these was a second Boxcar Children book. It was called *Surprise Island*.

In 1950, Warner turned 60 years old. She had been teaching for 32 years. She taught about 1,600 students during that time. She decided it was time to retire.

Now, Warner had more time for writing and volunteering. She joined the Connecticut Cancer Society and continued her work with the **Red Cross**. Sometimes, she wrote stories about what the workers were doing.

Warner also continued writing Boxcar Children books. Some of the next titles were *The Yellow House Mystery* and *Mystery Ranch*.

Health problems struck Warner again in 1959. She broke her hip one month before her fifth Boxcar Children **manuscript** was due. But, she met her **deadline** anyway.

Warner composed her stories in notebooks. Early on, she wrote her manuscripts in pencil. Later, she used thin-tipped black markers.

A House of Her Own

Warner never married. She joked that her brother and sister had married her best friends, so there was no one left for her. She lived in her parents' home for almost 40 years.

Later on, she moved to her grandmother's house. She moved again in 1962 to her own little brown-**shingled** home in Putnam. Warner said her home sat among "woods and good neighbors."

The little house became a popular spot for children. Many of Warner's fans came to visit her. They liked to come as soon as they had read the newest Boxcar Children book.

Warner wrote mostly about the Boxcar Children in her later years. One book was different, though. *Peter Piper, Missionary Parrot* was about a bird. The bird traveled with a minister. The book followed the adventures the two had in their many travels.

Warner continued to struggle with poor health. She had an elevator put in her home because she could not climb the stairs. In 1974, she broke her other hip. Despite her health problems, she always found ways to stay in touch with her readers.

Warner had always loved violets. In her writing workroom, she hung wallpaper with violets on it.

The Story Lives On

Warner was an important part of Putnam throughout her life. A local group gave her the Woman of the Year Award in 1965. Two years later, she accepted an award from the **Red Cross**. She had been a volunteer for 50 years.

In 1978, Warner received another honor. The library at the local elementary school was named after her. Unfortunately, she was not able to attend the **dedication** ceremony. She watched it on videotape instead.

Gertrude Chandler Warner died on August 30, 1979. She had been sick for a long time prior to her death. People in Putnam and around the world were saddened by the news. Warner touched many lives in her 89 years.

Warner wrote 19 Boxcar Children books. After her death, some readers feared there wouldn't be any more stories. Warner's publisher continued to get mail from young readers. They wanted to read more about the Alden children.

In 1991, Warner's publisher arranged for new authors to begin writing the books. The new writers had to remain true to Warner's vision for the series. Today, there are nearly 100 Boxcar Children adventure books. They are enjoyed by readers young and old.

After Warner's death, other authors continued to write Boxcar Children books. The popular children's series is available at most libraries.

Glossary

bedridden - having to stay in bed because of illness or injury.

bronchitis - a sickness that affects the lungs.

deadline - a date or time when something has to be completed.

dedication - a ceremony held to recognize someone's accomplishments.

depot - a train or bus station.

manuscript - a book or article written by hand or typed before being published.

Red Cross - an international organization that cares for the sick, wounded, or homeless.

shingle - a small, thin piece of material used to cover the roof or sides of a building in overlapping rows.

tutor - a person who privately teaches a student.

World War I - from 1914 to 1918, fought in Europe. Great Britain, France, Russia, the United States, and their allies were on one side. Germany, Austria-Hungary, and their allies were on the other side.

Web Sites

To learn more about Gertrude Chandler Warner, visit ABDO Publishing Company on the World Wide Web at **www.abdopub.com**. Web sites about Gertrude Chandler Warner are featured on our Book Links page. These links are routinely monitored and updated to provide the most current information available.

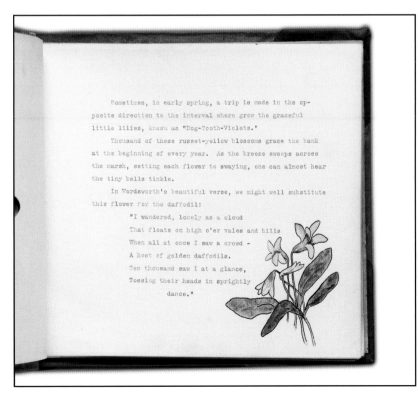

Warner loved wildflowers and often wrote about them.

Index